NASHVILLE PUBLIC LIBRARY

FOUNDATION

THE STORY OF
Soul and R&B

POP HISTORIES

MATT ANNISS

A+

Smart Apple Media

Published in the United States by Smart Apple Media
PO Box 3263, Mankato, Minnesota 56002

Copyright © 2014 Arcturus Publishing Limited

The right of Matt Anniss to be identified as the author of this work has been asserted by him in accordance with the Copyright, Designs and Patents Act 1988.

Text: Matt Anniss
Editors: Joe Harris and Rachel Blount
Design: Paul Myerscough and Keith Williams

Picture credits:
Corbis: Bettmann 11c, Michael Ochs Archives 6, 7t, Neal Preston 11t, 12, Lynn Goldsmith 16, 17b; Dreamstime: American Spirit 4t; Library of Congress: Ed Ford 13, Carol M. Highsmith 10, William P. Gottlieb Collection 4b; Philadelphia International Records: 14, 15; Shutterstock: David Adamson 9c, Arvzdix 17t, S Bukley 11b, 23, 25, Elizabeth Dover 31, Helga Esteb 19b, 27t, Featureflash 7b, 9b, 18, 19t, 26, 27b, 29b, Gustavo Miguel Fernandes 21, Mat Hayward 20, Patricia Marks 9t, Pjhpix 29t, Denise Richardson 1, 24, Debby Wong 5, 28; Visad Records: 22; Wikipedia: CBS Television 8.
Cover images: Shutterstock: David Adamson top center left, Elizabeth Dover main, top far right, Gustavo Miguel Fernandes top right, miqu77 top left, Dana Nalbandian top center right; Wikipedia: Nationaal Archief top far left.

Library of Congress Cataloging-in-Publication Data

Anniss, Matt.
 The story of soul and R&B / Matt Anniss.
    pages cm. -- (Pop histories)
 Includes index.
 Summary: "Describes the beginnings and evolution of Soul and R&B music, spotlighting important artists and songs"--Provided by publisher.
 ISBN 978-1-59920-966-1 (library binding)
 1. Soul (Music)--History and criticism--Juvenile literature. 2. Rhythm and blues (Music)--History and criticism--Juvenile literature. I. Title.

 ML3537.A56 2014
 781.644--dc23
                          2013003609

Printed in China

SL002674US

Supplier 03, Date 0513, Print Run 2378

CONTENTS

THE ROOTS OF SOUL

Today, many of the world's most famous singers and performers come from a soul or rhythm and blues (R & B) background. Yet it wasn't always this way. Sixty years ago, soul didn't even exist as a music style.

A BOOM IN THE POPULARITY OF RADIO STATIONS IN THE 1920S AND 1930S HELPED SPREAD THE GOSPEL SOUND FAR BEYOND ITS CHURCH ROOTS.

Church Music

The roots of soul and R & B can be found in religion and specifically in the African-American tradition of singing in church. In the early part of the twentieth century, a style of church music called gospel developed.

Different Style

Traditionally, the music sung in churches was sedate and serious. Gospel was anything but sedate. The songs were an upbeat celebration of the singers' belief in God and the Christian faith.

THE SINGING STYLE OF JAZZ PERFORMER BILLIE HOLLIDAY WAS A HUGE INFLUENCE ON EARLY GOSPEL GROUPS.

TESTIFY!

Gospel soon became hugely popular within African-American communities. From the 1930s onward, many top singers honed their skills by singing in church gospel choirs.

Gospel Beginnings

To this day, gospel remains a starting point for many top soul and R & B stars. Beyoncé, Chris Brown, Usher, and Alicia Keys all got a start in music by singing with their local church choir.

Two Become One

At some point in the 1950s, the paths of gospel-influenced doo-wop and raucous rhythm and blues crossed. When the two styles mingled, something new emerged. This fusion would become known as soul music.

Shooby Doo-wop

By the 1950s, many gospel singers had become "doo-wop" stars. Doo-wop used many of the same singing techniques as gospel, but its subject matter was less religious. Doo-wop songs talked about love and relationships rather than God and faith.

USHER IS JUST ONE OF MANY MODERN R & B STARS WHO DISCOVERED THEIR LOVE OF SINGING THROUGH THEIR MEMBERSHIP OF A CHURCH GOSPEL CHOIR.

The Roots of Rock and Roll

At the same time as doo-wop became popular, another form of black music, rhythm and blues, was beginning to make its mark. Louder, heavier, and more suitable for dancing, R & B was the inspiration for rock and roll music.

THE FIRST SOUL STARS

During the 1950s, two genuine stars emerged from the gospel, doo-wop, and rhythm and blues scenes. Between them, Ray Charles and Sam Cooke laid the foundations for the global pop success of soul stars in the decades to come.

Difficult Beginnings

Ray Charles Robinson went blind at the age of seven. He started learning to sing and play the piano while at school. He showed great talent, and at the age of 15, he started appearing with local bands.

Chance to Shine

Charles wasn't just a talented singer and musician, he was also a songwriter. In 1953, Atlantic Records offered him a recording contract. He was given the chance to record his own songs.

GENIUS AT WORK

It was Charles' songs that made him a huge star. Unlike many of his rivals, the blind musician wrote songs that combined elements of gospel, rhythm and blues, jazz, and pop. Out of this melting pot of styles came some of the first soul songs ever recorded.

IN 1960, RAY CHARLES WON HIS FIRST GRAMMY AWARD FOR HIS SINGLE *GEORGIA ON MY MIND*.

Star Potential

Sam Cooke was different to Ray Charles. Unlike Charles, Cooke looked like a star. He was also a smart businessman and knew that he could make money if he recorded the right songs. Ultimately, his impact on the emerging soul scene would be huge.

Change of Direction

Cooke made his name as a gospel singer and songwriter with the Soul Stirrers, but in 1957, he decided to record pop songs that combined doo-wop and rhythm and blues sounds. It was a smart move. His first big hit, *You Send Me*, reached the top of the charts in 1957.

Superstar

Between 1956 and 1963, Cooke recorded over 20 hit songs. His distinct style of "soulful" singing influenced many musicians in the fast-growing soul scene. His success paved the way for a new generation of soul stars to take to the stage.

BETWEEN 1957 AND 1964, SAM COOKE RECORDED 30 TOP 40 HITS, MAKING HIM THE MOST SUCCESSFUL AFRICAN-AMERICAN PERFORMER OF THE TIME.

SOUL HEROES

MICHAEL JACKSON ON RAY CHARLES

"His music is timeless, his contribution to the music industry unequaled and unparalleled. He paved the way for so many of us."

Michael Jackson (pictured)

THE HIT FACTORY

As the 1950s came to a close, soul was on the verge of a major breakthrough. With Ray Charles and Sam Cooke riding high in the charts, the time was right for a second wave of soul artists to push the new soul sound worldwide.

Berry Good Idea

One man saw this as a great opportunity. Berry Gordy was a failed musician but a shrewd businessman. He thought that soul music had potential to appeal to both black and white audiences.

DURING THE PEAK OF THEIR SUCCESS IN THE MID 1960S, MOTOWN GROUP THE SUPREMES WERE ALMOST AS POPULAR AS THE BEATLES.

Welcome to Hitsville

In 1959, Gordy put his plan into action. In his hometown of Detroit, he built a recording studio that he called "Hitsville U.S.A.". At the same time, he also launched two record labels, Tamla and Motown.

TOP TEAM

Gordy got together with a group of great local songwriters and musicians and set out to make pop hits. He signed up record producer Norman Whitfield and a talented songwriting team named Holland-Dozier-Holland.

The Motown Sound

Between them, Gordy and his team developed a slick, upbeat style of soul that quickly became known as the "Motown sound". This sound soon became popular with African-American and white teenagers, as Gordy predicted.

Big Hits

Motown's first big hit single was the Marvelettes' *Please Mister Postman*. It hit the top of the American pop charts in 1961. In the years that followed, Motown artists would dominate the pop charts worldwide.

Soul Legends

During the 1960s, the Motown "hit factory" was responsible for launching the careers of many soul legends, including Diana Ross, Stevie Wonder, Smokey Robinson, Marvin Gaye, the Temptations, and late in 1969, the Jackson 5.

BRITISH SINGER DUFFY IS ONE OF A NUMBER OF MODERN STARS WHO HAVE RECORDED HITS IN THE FAMOUS 1960S MOTOWN STYLE.

Lasting Legacy

In the years to come, Motown would become the most important soul record label of all time. The Motown sound continues to inspire musicians today. In recent years, Cee Lo Green, Beyoncé, Duffy, and Mayer Hawthorne have all recorded hits that influenced by Motown's 1960s soul.

LIVING LEGEND

STEVIE WONDER

Stevie Wonder recorded his first songs for Motown in 1961, when he was just 11 years old. Still recording today, he is one of the most celebrated soul musicians and songwriters of all time. Over a 50-year career, he has recorded many great records in a variety of styles, from disco and jazz to reggae and dance music.

9

FUNK BROTHERS AND SOUL SISTERS

On the back of Motown's success in the early 1960s, soul music entered a boom period. While the label's artists continued to dominate the pop charts, a new wave of soul performers began to take the music in new directions.

Sound of the City

Across America, distinctive soul scenes developed around certain cities. In Chicago, singer, songwriter, and record producer Curtis Mayfield was responsible for a musically rich style called "sweet soul".

DOWN SOUTH

Despite soul's roots in the northern United States, many of the most important developments of the period happened hundreds of miles away in the South.

FAME Game

FAME Studios in Alabama played a key role in the story of 1960s soul. It was there that Aretha Franklin, who would go on to become "the Queen of Soul", recorded her greatest hits.

Stax of Hits

The FAME sound, and that of nearby Stax Records, was different to the pop-friendly Motown sound. It was punchier, heavier, and had more in common with rhythm and blues. It was characterized by greater use of horns—brass instruments such as trumpets and saxophones.

THE FORMER HEADQUARTERS OF STAX RECORDS IN MEMPHIS, TENNESSEE, IS NOW HOME TO THE MUSEUM OF AMERICAN SOUL MUSIC.

Enter the Godfather

At the same time as Aretha Franklin and FAME's Muscle Shoals Rhythm Section were revolutionizing soul, another Southern performer was taking the sound in another direction. His name was James Brown, the self-styled "Godfather of Soul".

ALTHOUGH HE CALLED HIMSELF THE GODFATHER OF SOUL", JAMES BROWN IS BETTER KNOWN FOR DEVELOPING A TOUGHER, DANCE FLOOR-FRIENDLY STYLE CALLED "FUNK".

ARETHA FRANKLIN PERFORMS WITH BACKUP SINGERS DURING A RECORDING OF THE TV PROGRAM *SOUL TRAIN*.

Ain't It Funky!

Brown called his style "funk". It featured looser rhythms and more complex musical arrangements. It was designed for dancing, and in the years to come, it would become almost as popular as more traditional soul music. By the start of the 1970s, soul had grown up.

SOUL HEROES

LL COOL J ON JAMES BROWN

"He broke down mental and social barriers and made it possible for me, a black kid from Queens, to stand in front of Presidents and say 'I'm black and proud.'"

LL Cool J (pictured)

MAKING A POINT

Life for many African Americans in the early 1970s was not great. The Vietnam War loomed large, there was trouble on the streets, and crime and poverty were rife. Soul music, once a celebration of love and life, began to reflect the dark mood at the heart of black America.

Unlikely Hero

The catalyst for this change in soul music was an unlikely hero. Marvin Gaye was one of soul's biggest pop stars, having risen to fame on the back of the 1960s Motown sound. Few thought that Gaye was capable of recording anything but sweet pop songs.

Troubled Times

Gaye had other ideas. By 1970, he was fed up with making pop records and depressed by the state of American life. He decided to write songs about his feelings and recorded what many believe is the greatest soul album of all time.

DEFINING MOMENT

Released in 1971, *What's Going On* changed the soul landscape forever. Written from the point of view of a soldier returning from Vietnam, it featured songs that discussed poverty, war, the environment, and life in America.

MARVIN GAYE TOOK A RISK BY MOVING INTO A MUCH DARKER SUBJECT MATTER IN THE 1970S, BUT THE PUBLIC EMBRACED HIS NEW, SOCIALLY AWARE STYLE.

SOUL MUSICIANS IN THE 1970S THOUGHT IT WAS THEIR DUTY TO WRITE SONGS ABOUT HOW TOUGH LIFE WAS FOR AFRICAN-AMERICAN CHILDREN IN U.S. CITIES.

Revolutionary Release

The music featured on *What's Going On* was different to anything that had come before. Produced by Gaye himself, it was much more intricate and detailed. Its mellow, bittersweet sound complemented the album's dark subject matter perfectly.

Just the Start

In the wake of *What's Going On*, many other soul performers recorded albums that tackled difficult and controversial subjects, such as drug use, violence, and life on the streets.

Socially Conscious

In the early 1970s, Sly and the Family Stone, Curtis Mayfield, and Stevie Wonder all recorded landmark albums that commented on African-American life. Marvin Gaye's masterpiece had ushered in a new era of socially conscious soul.

PLAYLIST
1970s SOCIAL SOUL

Marvin Gaye—*Inner City Blues (Makes Me Wanna Holler)* (Motown, 1971)

Curtis Mayfield—*Little Child Running Wild* (Custom, 1972)

Bobby Womack—*Across 110th Street* (United Artists, 1972)

Stevie Wonder—*Living for the City* (Tamla, 1973)

Gil Scott-Heron & Brian Jackson—*The Bottle* (Strata-East Records, 1974)

THE SOUND OF PHILADELPHIA

Until 1971, the city of Philadelphia had very little musical history. Yet by the middle of the 1970s, the city was at the center of a soul revolution. From nowhere, the "Philly sound" had conquered the world.

Philadelphia International

In 1971, a trio of Philadelphia-based songwriters, Kenneth Gamble, Leon Huff, and Thom Bell, decided to found their own record label. Called Philadelphia International Records, it would release music recorded at the city's Sigma Sound Studios.

SOUL SOUNDS

At the heart of the Philadelphia International sound was a group of 30 musicians known as MFSB (Mother, Father, Sister, Brother). Effectively a "soul orchestra", MFSB would provide the backing music for all of the label's releases.

Upbeat Alternative

In contrast to the socially conscious soul style of the time, the music released by Philadelphia International acts such as the O'Jays, Billy Paul, Harold Melvin and the Blue Notes, and the Three Degrees was upbeat and luscious. It offered a rich, expansive alternative to the grittiness often found in other soul records.

PHILADELPHIA INTERNATIONAL SONGWRITERS AND MUSIC PRODUCERS GAMBLE & HUFF WERE ADDED TO THE DANCE MUSIC HALL OF FAME IN 2005 IN HONOR OF THEIR CONTRIBUTION TO SOUL AND DISCO.

Important Record

The record that defined the Philly soul sound was recorded by MFSB in 1973. *TSOP (The Sound of Philadelphia)* became famous as the theme tune to America's number one soul television program, *Soul Train*. Unlike most Philly Sound releases, it had no words; it was an instrumental track.

Dance Music

TSOP became popular with dancers in nightclubs. With its relentless beat, big horns, and sweeping orchestral strings (a combination of violins, violas, and cellos), it would become the blueprint for a whole new style of dance floor-friendly soul: disco.

The Shape of Things to Come

To begin with, disco was just a name given to a loose style of music played in the underground nightclubs of New York City. Initially, much of that music had been made in Philadelphia. Soon, though, disco would become a worldwide phenomenon.

THE BACK COVER OF MFSB'S CLASSIC ALBUM *LOVE IS THE MESSAGE* FEATURED PICTURES OF THE MANY DIFFERENT MUSICIANS INVOLVED IN GAMBLE AND HUFF'S SOUL ORCHESTRA.

INSIDE THE SOUND
PHILLY SOUL

The Philly Sound was different to what had come before for a number of reasons. First, it combined elements of traditional funk and soul with musical arrangements influenced by the looseness of jazz. The use of an orchestra on almost all releases was also new to soul, while the steady, high-speed backbeat made it perfect for dancing.

YOU SHOULD BE DANCING

In the mid to late 1970s, disco was everywhere. Inspired by the lush Philly Sound, soul musicians across the world began making more and more records designed to thrill nightclub dancers.

THE SOUND OF THE CITY

The center of the disco universe was New York City. It was here that the style had first emerged, as DJs entertained clubbers with a mix of Philly Sound, funk, and dance floor-friendly rock records. By the mid 1970s, a distinct New York disco style had emerged.

Celebrate Life

Disco was not about commenting on the state of the world but rather about celebrating life. Its songs were fun, upbeat, and perfect to dance to.

Salsoul Man

New York was also home to the most influential disco record labels of the period. They included Salsoul—whose orchestra was conducted by former MFSB member Vincent Montana, West End, and Prelude.

KOOL AND THE GANG WERE ONE OF THE MOST SUCCESSFUL BANDS OF THE DISCO ERA.

Good Times

It wasn't long before disco songs were scaling the pop charts. Kool and the Gang, Chic, and KC and the Sunshine Band became massive stars on the back of radio-friendly disco hits. Even soul legends Marvin Gaye and Stevie Wonder recorded disco records.

Night Fever

In 1977, disco went worldwide thanks to a hit movie called *Saturday Night Fever*. The soundtrack album, featuring disco songs by the Bee Gees, is still one of the best-selling records of all time.

The Birth of a Superstar

Already a huge pop star with his brothers in the Jackson 5, Michael Jackson became one of the biggest stars of the disco era. He was 21 when he recorded his first disco album, *Off the Wall*, in 1979. Over the next 20 years, he would record countless number one singles.

Death of Disco

The success of disco couldn't last. By the early 1980s, times had changed and the public was sick of disco music. For soul to survive, it would have to reinvent itself once again.

THE KING OF POP, MICHAEL JACKSON, PERFORMS WITH THE JACKSON 5 DURING THEIR 1984 *VICTORY* TOUR.

RIP IT UP AND START AGAIN

By the early 1980s, interest in soul music was dwindling. The demise of disco and the rise of fresh new musical styles such as hip-hop and electronic pop showed soul musicians the way forward. Change was needed—and fast.

Synthesizer Age

All the new styles of music attracting listeners had one thing in common: They all used electronic instruments, such as synthesizers (keyboards) and drum machines. Listeners wanted music that sounded like the future, not the past.

Blame It on the Boogie

Soul music producers and performers embraced this change, first by using these instruments in dance music productions. This style was known as "boogie" or "electrofunk". It retained the dance floor spirit of disco but gave it a futuristic twist.

Birth of R & B

Contemporary R & B was nothing like rhythm and blues. It was based around tight drum machine rhythms, futuristic synthesizer sounds, and slick, soulful vocals. It quickly became hugely popular and laid the foundations for the dominance of today's R & B artists.

JANET JACKSON, SISTER OF SOUL LEGEND MICHAEL, WAS ONE OF THE FIRST STARS OF CONTEMPORARY R & B.

Massive Stars

By the mid 1980s, contemporary R & B artists were enjoying hits across the globe. Whitney Houston, Luther Vandross, Loose Ends, and Cherelle all became stars on the back of hot R & B productions.

Introducing Jam & Lewis

The genius of contemporary R & B was that it was extremely soulful but also appealed to listeners brought up on electronic pop. The masters of the sound were a pair of music producers, Jimmy Jam and Terry Lewis.

R & B Heroes

Jam and Lewis were hugely important figures in contemporary R & B. Their productions for Janet Jackson, the SOS Band, and Alexander O'Neal became huge hits. They continue to be important figures in R & B today and have produced albums for Usher and Mariah Carey.

LUTHER VANDROSS FIRST MADE HIS NAME AS AN UNDERGROUND DISCO SINGER, BEFORE GOING ON TO BE ONE OF THE BIGGEST SOUL STARS OF THE 1980S.

○ PLAYLIST
1980s R & B

Luther Vandross—*Never Too Much*
(Epic Records, 1981)

The SOS Band—*Just Be Good to Me*
(Tabu Records, 1983)

Cherelle featuring Alexander O'Neal—*Saturday Love* (Tabu Records, 1985)

Loose Ends—*Hanging on a String (Contemplating)* (Virgin Records, 1985)

Janet Jackson – *What Have You Done for Me Lately?* (A&M Records, 1986)

JIMMY JAM AND TERRY LEWIS WERE ARGUABLY THE MOST INFLUENTIAL MUSIC PRODUCERS OF THE 1980S.

BLUE-EYED SOUL

While contemporary R & B was revitalizing soul in the 1980s, another trend was emerging. Away from black communities, white artists were making music inspired by classic soul hits. This became known as "blue-eyed soul", and it was massive.

1960s Roots

Blue-eyed soul was not a new thing. During the 1960s, a number of white artists such as The Righteous Brothers and Dusty Springfield became stars on the back of a sound that was heavily influenced by Motown and Stax styles.

You Should Be Dancing

Blue-eyed soul continued to grow in prominence in the 1970s, with Boz Scaggs, the Average White Band, and the Bee Gees all recording hits inspired by soul. Even David Bowie tried his hand at blue-eyed soul with the *Young Americans* album.

BLUE-EYED STARS

By the 1980s, blue-eyed soul had become an established style, with stars to match. The record that started it all was Hall & Oates' 1981 hit *I Can't Go for That (No Can Do)*. Interestingly, it got just as much airplay on American contemporary R & B radio stations as on rock stations.

DARYL HALL AND JOHN OATES WERE AMONG THE PIONEERS OF THE BLUE-EYED SOUL SOUND, WHICH REMAINS HUGELY POPULAR TODAY.

Rock and Soul

Hall & Oates were the undisputed stars of the blue-eyed soul movement. They began their career pushing a style they described as "rock and soul". By the 1980s, they'd dropped most of their rock influences and were making a smooth, radio-friendly style of soul that appealed to both black and white audiences.

Follow-Up Fits

In the wake of Hall & Oates's success, many white artists recorded songs directly influenced by soul. George Michael, Michael McDonald, Robert Palmer, and Simply Red all scored hits with blue-eyed soul songs.

Modern Movement

Today, blue-eyed soul remains popular. In recent years, Mayer Hawthorne, Christina Aguilera, and Joss Stone have all recorded pop hits that are directly influenced by classic soul sounds from the 1960s and 1970s.

PLAYLIST
BLUE-EYED SOUL

Dusty Springfield—*Don't Forget about Me* (Atlantic Records, 1969)

Boz Scaggs – *Lowdown* (Columbia, 1976)

Hall & Oates—*I Can't Go for That (No Can Do)* (RCA Victor, 1981)

Peter Gabriel—*Sledgehammer* (Virgin Records, 1986)

Mayer Hawthorne—*No Strings* (Stones Throw Records, 2011)

SWING THING

R& B as we know it today bears little relation to the contemporary R & B style of the mid 1980s. But the distinctive sound of modern soul records can be traced back to the 1980s and a style called "new jack swing".

Fresh Beats

Riley quickly became an in-demand producer. On tracks by Keith Sweat, Johnny Kemp, and Bobby Brown, he tried out a new style, mixing contemporary gospel-influenced R & B vocals with hip-hop beats. It was a revelation.

Teddy Boy

The architect of the new jack swing style was a musician, performer, and producer named Teddy Riley. During the mid 1980s, he got his break producing hip-hop records for the likes of Doug E. Fresh, Heavy D and the Mob, and Kool Moe Dee.

NEW JACK SWING

In 1987, Riley formed a band called Guy in order to develop his new sound further. A year later, in 1988, a magazine article about Riley and Guy described the music as "new jack swing". The name stuck.

HIP-HOP BEATMAKER TURNED MUSIC PRODUCER TEDDY RILEY (PICTURED HERE, WITH STEVIE WONDER ON THE LEFT) ALMOST SINGLE-HANDEDLY CREATED THE MODERN R & B SOUND WITH HIS NEW JACK SWING STYLE.

"Go-To" Man

In the early 1990s, Teddy Riley's fusion of soul and hip-hop became the dominant form of R & B. Riley was the go-to producer for soul artists in search of a hit. He worked with Michael Jackson and enjoyed success with his own hip-hop/R & B act, Blackstreet.

Puffy and Babyface

Many other producers followed in Riley's footsteps and enjoyed great success. Among the most notable are Babyface, who launched the careers of Usher and TLC, and Sean Combs, later to find fame as P. Diddy. Before embarking on a solo career, he produced R & B hits for Faith Evans, Jodeci, and Boyz II Men.

Critical Style

New jack swing was an important development. It cemented the relationship between hip-hop and soul that exists to this day. Without new jack swing, R & B as we know it would not exist.

INSIDE THE SOUND

NEW JACK SWING

New jack swing was unique at the time because it fused the swinging, often slow beats of hip-hop (and occasionally the raps, too) with soul vocals. Musically, it also borrowed from pop, jazz, and contemporary R & B dance music. The result was something that sounded like nothing else around.

IN THE 1990S, MUSIC PRODUCER BABYFACE WAS ONE OF THE MOST IN-DEMAND MEN IN R & B THANKS TO HIS WORK WITH USHER AND TLC.

BRAND NEO

As the 1990s continued, many younger soul musicians began to tire of the slick, poppy R & B songs that dominated the charts. Instead, they looked to the past for inspiration, creating a new style that became known as "neo soul".

Soul to Neo Soul

Neo soul actually had its roots in the late 1980s and early '90s, when groups such as Tony! Toni! Tone! and Soul II Soul blended classic soul elements with contemporary R & B, hip-hop, and funk influences.

Paying Tribute

These acts shared a desire to make music that was modern but looked to the past for inspiration. Both acts were known for making music that used samples (extracts from previous recordings) by classic soul and funk acts.

SOCIAL SOUL REVIVAL

In the mid 1990s, a new wave of soul acts inspired by the past as much as the present began to emerge. D'Angelo, Maxwell, Lauren Hill, and Erykah Badu led the way, releasing albums that recalled the glory days of 1970s socially conscious soul while sounding thoroughly modern.

DESPITE TELLING JOURNALISTS THAT SHE HATED THE TERM NEO SOUL, ERYKAH BADU DID MUCH TO POPULARIZE THE STYLE IN THE 1990S.

Fitting Name

Although many of the artists didn't like it, music critics started describing their style as neo soul. Since the musicians involved put greater emphasis on songwriting and complex musical arrangements—as Stevie Wonder, Curtis Mayfield, and Marvin Gaye had done in the 1970s—it seemed fitting.

Big Impact

Neo soul had a profound impact on the R & B scene. It showed that there was a market for intelligent, thoughtful music that blended the latest beats and production techniques with classic sounds and proper instruments.

Modern Soul

In the wake of neo soul, an underground "modern soul" movement began to develop around the world. Artists felt as if they could express themselves, rather than worry about chasing pop hits. Today, modern soul continues to thrive away from the mainstream.

PHARRELL WILLIAMS FIRST FOUND FAME AS PART OF MUSIC PRODUCTION OUTFIT THE NEPTUNES BUT LATER WENT ON TO BECOME A STAR IN HIS OWN RIGHT AS A NEO SOUL SINGER.

PLAYLIST
NEO SOUL & MODERN SOUL

Soul II Soul – *Keep on Movin'*
(10 Records, 1989)

D'Angelo—*Brown Sugar* (EMI, 1995)

Erykah Badu—*On & On*
(Kedar/Universal, 1997)

Raphael Saadiq & Q-Tip—*Get Involved*
(Hollywood Records, 1999)

Pharrell feat Jay-Z—*Frontin'*
(Star Trak Entertainment, 2003)

R&B GOES GLOBAL

Neo soul proved that there was still a market for intelligent soul music. Meanwhile, swing and hip-hop-influenced R & B continued to thrive. As the 1990s drew to a close, R & B was the dominant force in pop music.

Pop Master Plan

The popularity of R & B made pop producers and record label owners sit up and take notice. They realized that R & B's mainstream appeal made it the perfect style for their pop acts.

R & B DESTINY

The tail end of the 1990s saw the emergence of a number of pop-R & B stars, most notably Destiny's Child. A girl group fronted by singer Beyoncé Knowles, they specialized in a style of music that blended catchy pop songs with the urban beats of R & B.

Destiny Calling

Backed by expensive music videos, Destiny's Child quickly became huge stars. After making waves with a traditional R & B song, *No, No, No*, they found international fame with the tracks *Say My Name* and *Bootylicious*.

During the late 1990s and early 2000s, R & B group Destiny's Child was one of the most popular pop acts on the planet.

26

Breakthrough Record

Bootylicious was a major breakthrough for R & B pop. It proved that music fans would respond to uptempo pop that blended R & B style vocals with danceable beats. It ushered in a new era of dance floor-friendly R & B pop.

Innovative Hit

After Destiny's Child split up, Beyoncé struck out on her own and became one of the biggest pop stars in the world. She continued to push forward an innovative, dance floor-friendly blend of R & B, pop, and hip-hop with 2003 single *Crazy in Love*. This upbeat song was built around a sample of the horn section from a 1970s soul record.

Global Stars

The success of Beyoncé paved the way for many more soul and pop performers to enjoy worldwide success. In recent years, Kelis, Tweet, Rihanna, Usher, Chris Brown, Justin Timberlake, and Kelly Rowland (one of Beyoncé's old Destiny's Child bandmates) have all enjoyed huge success with catchy R & B pop songs.

MANY OF THE WINNERS OF SIMON COWELL'S TV TALENT SHOWS, SUCH AS THE *X FACTOR* AND *AMERICA'S GOT TALENT*, HAVE ENJOYED BIG HITS WITH SONGS THAT BLEND ELEMENTS OF R & B AND POP.

LIVING LEGEND

BEYONCÉ

Beyoncé Knowles formed her own girl group while still at school, but she found little success until Destiny's Child, her second band, were signed to Columbia Records in 1997. Since then, Beyoncé has become a huge star in her own right and was one of the top-selling pop acts of the 2000s. She married rapper Jay-Z in 2008.

BIG BUSINESS

In the twenty-first century, soul and R & B are very big business. Having started as an offshoot of gospel in black communities, they have become the biggest musical force on the planet. They have also made a lot of people very rich.

Fashion Lines

Beyoncé, arguably the soul scene's biggest pop star of recent years, has followed the lead of hip-hop stars such as her husband Jay-Z by expanding into business. She has her own range of perfumes and fragrances and a fashion clothing company.

ENTER RIHANNA

Beyoncé is not alone. Rihanna is another R & B performer who has used her name and reputation to launch a range of fragrances. Now, top R & B and soul stars regularly exploit their "brand" by starting fashion companies.

Multimillionaires

The pulling power of top R & B and soul stars can be seen in their dominance of the live circuit. In 2011, Rihanna embarked on a huge global tour. It helped her to earn a reported $53 million between March 2011 and April 2012, making her one of the richest pop stars on the planet.

RIHANNA HAS BEEN PRESENTED WITH MANY AWARDS, INCLUDING FIVE GRAMMIES AND FIVE AMERICAN MUSIC AWARDS.

Festival Favorites

Even music festivals, usually the preserve of rock stars, have fallen in love with R & B and soul. In 2011, Beyoncé performed at some of the world's top festivals, including Glastonbury in the UK.

Soul Revival

While R & B stars continue to dominate the pop charts, traditional soul, based on the sounds of the 1960s and 1970s, has made a comeback. In recent years, Mayer Hawthorne, Cee Lo Green, and Duffy have all recorded huge hits inspired by classic soul.

Fast-Forward to the Future

R & B and soul continues to look forward, too. Recent hits by top stars have included collaborations with top dance music producers such as David Guetta, and hip-hop stars including Snoop Dogg, Jay-Z, and P. Diddy. Soul and R & B remain in great health.

R & B AND SOUL ACTS ARE OFTEN ASKED TO HEADLINE MUSIC FESTIVALS AROUND THE WORLD.

LIVING LEGEND

RIHANNA

Robyn Rihanna Fenton was born in Barbados in 1988. She got her big break when she met an American record producer in 2004. Within a year, she'd signed a record deal and was on the fast track to stardom. To date, her songs have been downloaded over 47 million times, making her one of the most successful singers of all time.

GLOSSARY

beats Rhythmic drumming.

collaboration The process of making something, for example, a song, with someone else.

communities Groups of people who live near each other.

contemporary Modern.

controversial Something that divides opinion and stirs up emotions.

distinctive Something that stands out or isn't like anything else.

drum machine An electronic instrument used to create drumbeats.

dwindling Becoming smaller or less popular.

embarking Starting on something, such as a career or a journey.

era A period of time.

fusion Putting two or more things together, such as styles of music, to make something new.

genuine Real, true.

hip-hop A style of music that features rapping over a steady beat.

influential Something that inspires people and changes their attitude or approach.

innovative Forward-thinking; usually used to describe something that is new and influential.

intricate Very detailed and complicated.

landmark In musical terms, a song or album of historical importance.

mainstream Popular.

masterpiece A term of praise given to songs or albums of historical importance.

mingled Joined together.

potential Future ability or possibility.

producer A person who oversees the recording of music.

prominent Something that stands out.

raucous Loud and unruly.

revitalizing Bringing back to life.

revolutionary Something that is so significant that it changes history or the way we think.

sample An extract from another song, often used in the making of hip-hop and R & B records.

synthesizer An electronic instrument, based on a piano.

underground Something that is not well known and usually popular only with a small group of people.

FURTHER INFORMATION

Further Reading

The History of Funk Music by Therlee Gipson (CreateSpace, 2012)

Ray Charles: I Was Born with Music Inside Me by Carin T. Ford (Enslow Publishers, 2007)

Rhythm & Blues, Rap & Hip-Hop by Frank Hoffmann and Albin J Zak (Checkmark Books, 2007)

Turn the Beat Around: The Secret History of Disco by Peter Shapiro (Faber & Faber, 2007)

Where Did Our Love Go? The Rise and Fall of the Motown Sound by Nelson George (University of Illinois Press, 2007)

Web Sites

www.discomusic.com
Learn more about the history of disco music and listen to classic songs.

http://www.soultracks.com
This superb web site features biographies and links for soul music artists, videos, news, and reviews on soul music old and new.

www.thisisrnb.com
Keep up to date with the R & B scene with news, interviews, and the latest videos.

www.top100sradio.com
Check out this web site and listen to the top 100 soul and R & B songs of all time, all picked by experts.

www.vibe.com
Investigate the web site of America's top R & B and hip-hop magazine founded by producer Quincy Jones, featuring news, reviews, and up-and-coming artists.

INDEX